JOB SEEKING WARRIORS

A Mentor's Guide to Winning

Richard D. Blumberg

First Printing, 2022

ISBN Paperback: 979-8-9852284-0-3

ISBN e-Book: 979-8-9852284-1-0

Library of Congress Control Number: 2021922408

For information about special discounts for bulk purchase or to bring the author to a live event, virtual session or classroom contact info@JobSeekingWarriors.com or visit www.JobSeekingWarriors.com.

Cover and Skillset layout designed by Carmel Monckton.
Page layout by Carmel Monckton.
Editing by Megan Okoniewski.

To my wife Sharon, daughter Lauren, and
son Steven who inspire me to seize each day
and make positive forward progress.

TABLE OF CONTENTS

THE PLEDGE

I will become whatever I want
to become.

I will leverage my skills, education,
and work experiences to the fullest.

I will work hard and smart to make
forward progress.

I will succeed by way of focus
and persistence.

I will pay the price to reach
my dreams.

I will achieve happiness and success.

I will pass it forward.

.... X SIGN HERE

THE JOB SEEKING WARRIOR'S SKILLSET

1: The Challenge

Power

Mission

Transition

Job Intelligence

Crossing Over

2: Developing Strategy

Begin Now

Overcome Fears

Position Strengths

Persistance

Don't Settle

3: Positioning for Triumph

Abundance

Hidden Opportunities

Tailor Your Resume

Plan

Build Your Brand

4: Proactive Engagement

Advantage

Networking

Fishing

Cover Letter

Follow Up

5: Pursuing a Position

3-Legged Stool

Top Economic Descision Maker

Gatekeeper

Informational Meeting

Foot in the Door

6: The Power to Win

Prepare

2-Way Interview

Salary Negotiation

Recieve an Offer

Mentor

PROLOGUE: THE JOB SEEKING WARRIOR'S SKILLSET

The Job Seeking Warrior embodies an aspiration for a comprehensive, holistic approach in pursuing a great professional position. Every job seeker can become a Job Seeking Warrior if they are willing to put in the time and effort.

This book is written in a style that appeals to both spatial and analytical thinkers. It can be read from start to finish, left to right; or it can be opened to select an applicable passage for consideration.

This book is purposely symmetrical: six chapters with five sections each worked out to share insights based on a specified arc, flow, and conciseness.

The book's spatial style addresses insightful topics in each section. In each chapter, the Job Seeking Warrior's Skillset is on the left page. The topic icon at hand is highlighted, while the others are lightened, but still in view, as it is important to see the skill at hand in context to the other attributes.

The analytical approach values connection to experiences by pinpointing the steps to achieve success along with a variety of examples throughout the book. As an analogy, it is about seeing the forest and examining a number of the trees. The Mentor shares experiences and invites the job seeker to further develop their own skillsets based on engagement with perspective employers, individuals, and groups.

Merriam-Webster Definitions

Spatial:
Relating to, or involved in the perception of relationships (as of objects) in space.

Analytical:
Separating something into component parts or constituent elements.

Each chapter includes a Checklist to encourage the job seeker to write down actionable next steps that can include one or more of the following: ideas, key activities, priorities, interests, dreams, skills, organizations, individuals, news/articles/posts, trends, and/or compelling issues.

When we write down our plans, and break them down into smaller next steps, it represents a way to say to the marketplace, *"I am ready to put in motion the activities needed to obtain a high-quality position."*

The job seeker is challenged to take a focused approach. To define and redefine situations from negative to positive, complex to simpler, and difficult to easier.

Each section includes a Checklist to encourage the job seeker to write down actionable next steps.

Job Seeking Warriors recognize the value of the spatial and analytics approach and uses this knowledge to take positive steps forward. They embrace directing their search and shaping their future.

ABOUT THE JOB SEEKING WARRIOR

Welcome to the jobs marketplace. A place where career opportunities constantly change.

As a mentor or coach, I am just like you, but have traveled a little bit longer and further on the career journey. I have persisted and wrestled along the way to acquire certain skills and expertise, which when used by the right job seeker (aka student, recent graduate, alumni, or experienced professional), can provide great value, benefit, and impact.

My goal is to teach and spread the knowledge of how to accelerate a quality job search wherever I can and have been doing so for decades.

Success from these activities is in the hands of the job seeker with a sincere interest to aspire to a great position, as well as tap into the power of preparation, passion, and persistence.

Aspiring candidates who seek quick fixes, shortcuts, and distraction from their circumstances will eventually find a job, but it may take longer, and they may settle for the wrong one.

As a result, the mindset of a Job Seeking Warrior becomes important to those individuals committed to taking action with a focus on their mission. They engineer their activities and mindset to find solutions every step of the way. They accept the responsibility to steer themselves in their chosen direction.

All job seekers can have trepidations at some point. They may overthink or second guess their actions. They must be prepared for the ups and downs that lie ahead, face challenges, setbacks, roadblocks, rejection, and in turn prepare, believe, and always move forward.

The Job Seeking Warrior has a mental toughness to reduce worrying and negative thoughts, and instead focus on goals and dreams. They continuously seek growth and improvement by learning and assessing what they can improve and taking calculated risks. They push themselves to be their best every day, exceed expectations, go outside their comfort zones, and find ways to contribute to the greater good.

Job Seeking Warriors cultivate:

- ➡ Integrity
- ➡ Belief
- ➡ Self-motivation
- ➡ Preparedness
- ➡ Resilience
- ➡ Energy
- ➡ Skills
- ➡ Discipline
- ➡ Persistence
- ➡ Effort
- ➡ Initiative
- ➡ Purpose
- ➡ Mindfulness
- ➡ Adaptability
- ➡ Decisiveness
- ➡ Creativity
- ➡ Innovation
- ➡ Winning

The aspiring Job Seeking Warrior has their work cut out for them but can absolutely achieve success.

The time-tested methods outlined in these chapters are designed for those who are ready to persevere, explore options, finetune, and energize their career to its highest potential.

To achieve their objectives, they take command of three challenges.

1. **Accepting accountability to themselves**
2. **Engaging organizations of interest**
3. **Interacting with peers, colleagues, experts, leaders, and influencers**

If you are ready to secure your next opportunity, then develop an approach that works for you. Set aside time to put a plan in motion. Write it down. Celebrate small and big victories along the way.

The job seeker looks for unexpected opportunities. They pursue a campaign approach and orchestrate multiple search activities simultaneously.

For the Job Seeking Warrior, the difference between success and failure starts with the simple decision to position strengths, as well as the determination to make progress one step a time.

THE VOW

How did the passion to share job, career, and professional development knowledge begin for the Mentor?

After graduation from his university, he traveled off and on for close to a year. He back-packed through Europe and returned home. Before the winter set in, he flew with a friend to Oahu, Hawaii, for what turned out to be two-and-a-half months of adventure.

Upon returning he was ready to find a job but was ill equipped to do so. While he had earned a degree in business and marketing there was still a lot to learn about the job market. He needed to take additional personal accountability to navigate toward a new opportunity and go beyond luck and circumstances.

The Mentor contacted a former professor who offered to teach him his principles of job seeking in four one-hour lessons at his house. That sounded fine, except for the price of $200.00 per hour, which was a lot of money back in the day. His father advised, *"If you can learn from his expertise, it will last you for your whole career, and it would be worth it."* He took two lessons and figured he had learned enough.

In short order, the Mentor found an Import Export job. After a few short months, the company moved to an industrial park. While he experienced a few interesting lessons about stevedores, truckers, importing and exporting steel and cement, and economic redevelopment, he knew he was in the wrong role and at a dead end at this stage of his career.

How could he have gone through a top university with so much promise and ended up in such a desolate place?

He was not the master of his own journey, which added to his frustration.

During a lunch break walk a flash went off in his head, and he made a vow.

If he could master the science and art of finding a job, he would share it with whomever would be interested to learn a concise, high-probability approach to success.

He would pass this knowledge forward if only he could learn the secrets.

Surely the path for finding a job existed. He asked everyone in his network for advice and insights but could not seem to find the answers. Yes, one person knew one part or another, but no one person seemed to be able to put the whole *"job seeking"* package together.

From that day forward he would do everything in his power to acquire the knowledge needed to target a high-quality position and win it.

And while it took close to two decades to confirm a level of mastery...

...he finally figured it out by passing his own test.

Years later, after delaying the launch of a consulting business when his father passed away, he decided to go on a job search and scored two offers for over six figures each. One from a *"cold call"* using a 3-pronged approach, and the other with the assistance of a recruiter.

In going through the job seeking cycle in about 45 days, he knew he was ready. He had finally mastered a methodology for how to find a job.

Along the way, he shared his career journey with an account executive who said, *"You no longer have to think about if you'll get a job, but rather what job you really want. Clearly you have mastered the process."* His kind words were appreciated.

A year later, after he started his own business development consulting organization, he realized that the same precepts held true. The job seeker needs to position four attributes:

1. **Skills**
2. **Education**
3. **Work Experiences**
4. **Accomplishments**

After all, there is just one difference between selling a product or service and getting a job. With job seeking, you sell yourself.

TIME TO WRITE IT DOWN

Over the years he helped many job seekers by way of mentoring, coaching, volunteering, blogs, webinars, career events, roundtables, panel discussions, speed networking programs, and encouragement.

Finally, years later several mentees who had used the Mentor's methods to attain success reconnected with him and shared a similar message. They said in their own way:

> *I understand now that everyone is capable of being a successful job seeker. Although many do not see a path forward to optimize our search, we all can take advantage of our skills, tools, and resources. I have learned from you the importance of setting a direction, practicing persistence and discipline, and making forward progress based on your career passion, one step at a time. It is important to never give up. Rejection and setbacks are opportunities to learn and continuously improve.*

The Mentor appreciated hearing this feedback and thought back to all the students and alumni who engaged in his suggestions, and those who merely looked for a quick fix.

Over the years he helped many job seekers by way of mentoring, coaching, volunteering, blogs, webinars, career events, roundtables, panel discussions, speed networking programs, and encouragement.

A few days later, another one of the former job seekers emailed the Mentor two separate messages. The first spoke of the wisdom shared and discovered along the journey.

The second was even more profound.

The mentee wrote, *"It's time to write your techniques down so others can benefit from them, and that we can explain them to other aspiring job seekers."*

The Mentor reflected, *"If one more job seeker benefits, it's worth it."*

And so, this book began.

Chapter One

THE CHALLENGE

THE JOB SEEKING WARRIOR'S SKILLSET

1: The Challenge

- Power
- Mission
- Transition
- Job Intelligence
- Crossing Over

2: Developing Strategy

- Begin Now
- Overcome Fears
- Position Strengths
- Persistance
- Don't Settle

3: Positioning for Triumph

- Abundance
- Hidden Opportunities
- Tailor Your Resume
- Plan
- Build Your Brand

4: Proactive Engagement

- Advantage
- Networking
- Fishing
- Cover Letter
- Follow Up

5: Pursuing a Position

- 3-Legged Stool
- Top Economic Descision Maker
- Gatekeeper
- Informational Meeting
- Foot in the Door

6: The Power to Win

- Prepare
- 2-Way Interview
- Salary Negotiation
- Recieve an Offer
- Mentor

01: HARNESSING THE POWER

The Job Seeking Warrior self-identifies as one who is ready to harness the power of taking action.

Those on the career journey have a remarkable capability to direct their own path. It is essential to assess and explore the realities of the marketplace based on three universal requirements that impact all industries, organizations, and positions:

It's important to recognize job market patterns just as we anticipate the flow of the seasons: winter, spring, summer, and fall. For example, the geodesic dome popularized by Spaceship Earth at Epcot in Walt Disney World Resort, Florida, which is formed of triangles, exemplifies interconnected patterns of the strongest geometrical shapes.

Organizations have patterns that can be readily assessed and turned into opportunities. The more we learn, the more we can earn.

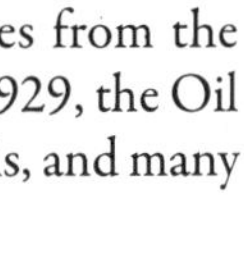

1. **Growing revenues**
2. **Improving operational efficiencies**
3. **Reducing costs**

Throughout history, job seekers have navigated through many economic crises from the COVID-19 pandemic to historic challenges spanning the Great Depression of 1929, the Oil Embargo of 1973, the 1981 Recession, the 9/11 attacks, the 2007 Mortgage Crisis, and many other peaks and valleys.

The job seeker acknowledges that they are not the first or last who will need to navigate through immense challenges to a great new opportunity. Once we gain greater awareness and make job seeking part of our daily ritual, we begin to develop a vision and identify a practical path forward as part of our career journey.

When the job seeker does not have a sense of control and/or does not recognize the patterns, they can become frustrated, fearful, impatient, apprehensive, and/or insecure.

For most, the key is to take positive, thoughtful steps toward one's goals.

When the job seeker does not have a sense of control and does not recognize the patterns, they can become frustrated, fearful, impatient, apprehensive, and/or insecure.

Consider the lesson of the Eiffel Tower. To get to the top using the elevator, riders require advance tickets and waiting in lines. Sometimes the elevator tickets for a given day are sold out. On the other hand, tickets to walk up the 1665 steps are readily available. A visitor must simply have a willingness to go up the steps one at a time and pursue the goal of getting to the top.

The job market acts in a similar way.

Job Seeking Warriors who are willing to invest in the extra effort of taking the steps, assessing the patterns, and following a process to achieve their objective have a higher success rate of landing an excellent job.

Forget about the fast lane. If you really want to fly, just harness your power to your passion.

- Oprah Winfrey

02: THE SIX FUNDAMENTALS OF THE MISSION

Job seekers must define a mission to help identify companies and individuals who share in similar values, principles, and to assess opportunities.

It is important to write down a mission statement representing a high-level view of what a job seeker wants and needs to do now to achieve their next job and impact their career. Creating one helps the job seeker focus on where they are going and what they are trying to accomplish, assess what success looks like, and guide decisions.

Steps for writing a career mission statement:

1. **Determine professional interests and passions.**
2. **Identify goals and objectives.**
3. **Pinpoint prior accomplishments, contributions, and strengths.**
4. **Position your skills, education, and work experiences.**
5. **Distinguish essential principles and values that are important.**
6. **Assess marketplace trends (e.g., growth, compelling business issues, innovation) and how you fit in.**

Developing a clear mission makes it easier to formulate a plan of action, set high standards, and stay on track. Each short-term gain along the way represents a stepping stone toward the main objective.

The Job Seeking Warrior must consider the following.

- **Recognize each challenge as an opportunity to learn and grow. Own it.**
- **Expect obstacles and rejection. Stay calm and find ways to overcome them.**
- **Embrace the process of getting a job or advancing one's career.**

Focus on planting the seeds of action, which will yield returns and position the seeker for longer-term, sustainable success.

The job challenge takes energy so use it wisely. Replenish it often.

For example, the Mentor connected with a job seeker who planned to take a job not aligned to any of the six fundamentals of the mission statement. The position was clearly a step backwards. With increased awareness they wrote down their objectives and went on a search more aligned to their career interests and ambitions.

The path to success requires intelligence, integrity, humility, resilience, endurance, and courage.

As a result, they redirected their course, which was worthy of their authentic self and would lead to a position in the Office of the CEO in their global organization.

The path to success requires intelligence, integrity, humility, resilience, endurance, and courage.

Celebrate every step of the journey.

Those who embrace these six fundamentals will be on their way to triumph.

Job Seeking Warriors assess their mission and take on the challenges of the road ahead. They continuously review their career path, job opportunities, goals, and mission statement and make adjustments along the way. They realize that as they make progress, self-confidence increases.

“ ”

To realize one's destiny is a person's only obligation.

- Paulo Coelho, The Alchemist

03: EXPERIENCING TRANSITIONS

Job Seeking Warriors experience transitions in their career journey. These changes along the way include both positive and negative encounters.

Transitions come in all shapes and sizes, whether as a student to a new intern (or co-op) position, a recent graduate, or a shift to a new job either as a promotion or horizontal move. Other transitions can include layoffs from downsizing, firings, or displacement and can be outright painful and unfair.

Three key considerations:

1. **Let go. Come to terms with your new or upcoming reality quickly.**
2. **Step back and assess the situation. Find calm.**
3. **Plan for new beginnings.**

Along the way the Mentor experienced a company-wide downsizing, which was an unexpected transition and major jolt.

When reaching out to friends and business colleagues about this frustrating setback he was asked,

"Is leaving a job or not having one a catastrophe?"

> Once a candidate realizes there is an abundance of opportunities and many jobs for the taking, then the process becomes more achievable.

There are many examples of catastrophes such as people who wake up every day without enough food for their families, who lose their home to a fire, or are in a car accident and experience unthinkable devastation.

Lacking a job (or the job you want) is temporary. Of course, we must pay our bills and keep a roof over our heads, but in context to a devastating catastrophe joblessness can be overcome.

With every career challenge, obstacle, or journey lies an opportunity to take the necessary steps forward.

Whether as a student, upcoming graduate, or a downsized or displaced worker, the potential to obtain a high-quality job exists. By following a thoughtful, consistent, disciplined approach, the Job Seeking Warrior has an excellent chance to achieve success.

The question: Are you willing to put in the effort, or do you want the easy way out?

Once a candidate realizes there is an abundance of opportunities and many jobs for the taking, then the process becomes more achievable.

The Job Seeking Warrior accepts accountability by recognizing and navigating through transitions.

“ ”

Any transition is easier if you believe in yourself and your talent.

- Priyanka Chopra

04: ACHIEVING JOB INTELLIGENCE

A Job Seeking Warrior recognizes the multifaceted nature of the career journey. Each action leads to greater goals. Each setback can slow the process and must be overcome.

Seeking a job can be incredibly stressful. The feeling of uneasiness or anxiety is normal. The key is to make adjustments, adapt to situations, listen more, and avoid personalizing the many obstacles that can arise.

Job intelligence helps the candidate recognize their own reactions, those of others, and make better decisions. It represents a set of skills and principles that helps with self-assessment, managing emotions, optimizing time, and harnessing one's purpose.

Job Seeking Warriors find ways to lift themselves up throughout the journey. They consider their inner S M A R R to find success in one or more of the following areas:

S = Spirit

M = Mind

A = Abilities

R = Relationships

R = Routine

The **Spirit** is shaped by faith and a connection to a higher power. The **Mind** reflects on the mental outlook, empathy, and tapping into one's emotions, which can have many ups and downs.

Abilities recognize that each seeker has unique talents that can contribute in a job and to the greater good. Building **Relationships** is essential to gaining informational insights, feedback, and referrals.

The **Routine** aspect of SMARR means to have a schedule; develop a consistent plan of action.

Stay disciplined to help ensure the desired results can be achieved...but they may take a bit longer than expected. Remember, *"Patience is a virtue"* that works best with a sense of urgency.

By developing the attributes of SMARR, the job seeker can reduce negative input and be in a better position to achieve their intended career goals.

Early in the Mentor's career, he was downsized by a Life Sciences Engineering, Construction, and Architecture firm after two years of supporting very large manufacturing plant deals. His first thoughts were disbelief and anger, but over time he realized that his knowledge of building pharmaceutical and biotechnology facilities was very limited, and it was better to take a new path.

Successful job seekers strive to be authentic. They are honest about their circumstances, and continuously evaluate their strengths and weaknesses, and position them in the best way.

This setback led to a successful career in the High Tech field. By first taking a temporary sales position, he developed the confidence to pursue a marketing position at a Fortune 500 technology firm, which resulted in being selected over ~200 applicants; many of them had more experience. Using the SMARR approach, even before he fully understood what it was all about, helped carve out a path grounded in focused planning, preparation, and constantly taking small steps forward.

During this pursuit, the Mentor began to make a life and work balance shift to avoid stress in the form of exercise, eating more healthy foods, developing hobbies, and practicing self-care to find peace and self-acceptance.

Over time the Mentor realized that while job seekers need help, they also should find ways to help others. For example, when they look to uncover jobs for other job seekers, versus only for themselves, as well as contribute as a volunteer and give back, they create more opportunities and have a higher rate of success.

Successful job seekers strive to be authentic. They are honest about their circumstances, and continuously evaluate their strengths and weaknesses, and position them in the best way.

With dedication, job seekers can become Job Seeking Warriors by using job intelligence strategies to help achieve their goals, increase awareness of their circumstance, maintain motivation, and build momentum centered on a positive outlook.

"

Knowing others is intelligence; knowing yourself is true wisdom.
Mastering others is strength; mastering yourself is true power.

- Lao Tzu, Tao Te Ching

05: GOING BEYOND THE CLIFF

Whenever the job seeker assesses their career...as a student, current professional, or displaced worker...they recognize they are at *"Point A"* and need to get to *"Point B"* to land the next job.

Job Seeking Warriors forge their path by developing great resilience. When faced with the challenge of getting a foot in the door and landing a job, they focus on positioning their strengths, targeting organizations and individuals of interest, and making tangible progress one step at a time.

Early in his career, the Mentor had the opportunity to have dinner with Geoffrey Moore, the acclaimed consultant and author of the book, "Crossing the Chasm." From this meeting, subsequent reading of his book, and many life experiences, the Mentor learned that there are times when we reach a point in business and/or our careers where we must cross a gap between where we are and where we want to be.

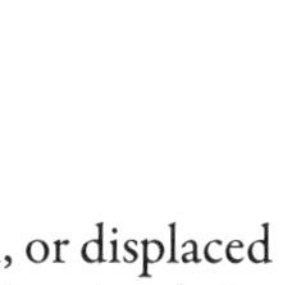

Think of a path where you come to the edge of a cliff and must cross to the cliff on the other side with a big drop-off in between. What if there was no way to get across? One would have to climb down...go over rocks and the terrain....in order to cross.

The Mentor learned that many individuals and groups get stuck along the way or never try to cross in the first place. Smart and tenacious job seekers figure out where there are opportunities, what it takes to gain progress, and set a strategy in motion to get to the other side.

The start of any job seeking venture begins with both challenges and some trepidation from entering into the unknown. There are a number of ways to gain a foothold by assessing:

1. **Who are the best target organizations and individuals?**
2. **What are the compelling trends that are driving hiring opportunities?**
3. **How do your strengths and weakness size up to job descriptions and**

hidden opportunities?

4. **Who in your alumni, professional, and personal network can help?**

5. **Who are the economic leaders, experts, managers who can influence hiring decisions?**

6. **What activities can help create a competitive advantage over other job seekers?**

The key to going from one cliff and getting to the other side is to engage in highly focused, targeted activities. Often the job seeker has an understanding of what they need to do but are unable or unwilling to put in the effort. They must fully commit to connecting their talent to what the organization is looking for based on the universal truths of driving revenue growth, operational efficiencies, and reducing costs.

While the path forward can have many ups and downs, it is important to strive toward a positive mindset. Thoughts of self-doubt should be reversed to taking concrete steps towards achieving goals.

While the path forward can have many ups and downs, it is important to strive toward a positive mindset.

Recognizing one's passion and playing into strengths will lead to the next opportunity.

The Job Seeking Warrior must assess where their skills and talents will be most valued and become the master of their own destiny.

" "

Obstacles don't have to stop you. If you run into a wall, don't turn around and give up. Figure out how to climb it, go through it, or work around it.

\- Michael Jordan

CHECKLIST

- [ ] ....

....

- [ ] ....

....

- [ ] ....

....

Chapter Two

DEVELOPING STRATEGY

THE JOB SEEKING WARRIOR'S SKILLSET

1: The Challenge

- Power
- Mission
- Transition
- Job Intelligence
- Crossing Over

2: Developing Strategy

- Begin Now
- Overcome Fears
- Position Strengths
- Persistance
- Don't Settle

3: Positioning for Triumph

- Abundance
- Hidden Opportunities
- Tailor Your Resume
- Plan
- Build Your Brand

4: Proactive Engagement

- Advantage
- Networking
- Fishing
- Cover Letter
- Follow Up

5: Pursuing a Position

- 3-Legged Stool
- Top Economic Descision Maker
- Gatekeeper
- Informational Meeting
- Foot in the Door

6: The Power to Win

- Prepare
- 2-Way Interview
- Salary Negotiation
- Recieve an Offer
- Mentor

06: THE POWER TO BEGIN

The proverb, *"The journey of a thousand miles begins with a first step"* from Lau Tzu's *Tao Te Ching*, reflects on the importance of patience, willpower, and determination in the face of a goal that may seem far away.

The job seeker does not have to do it all at once. By taking the first step, they gain confidence and motivation to make progress on an often challenging path.

Procrastination or a partial search will not lead to success or bring the job seeker closer to achieving their ambitions.

For many, the first step of approaching the unknown can be the most difficult. It's important to move forward even without the perfect situation, or that all the required skills or work experiences are in place.

The key is to learn, act, and take initiative.

Success is based on believing in the desired objective, accepting that there will be obstacles, and making steady progress.

The Mentor always asks a job seeker, *"Have you begun the search?"*

They frequently answer, *"Yes, I've posted on countless job boards"* and perhaps taken a few other steps.

As a result, the Mentor often hears the following feedback from the job seeker.

- **Not getting the interviews or jobs they want**
- **Settling for the jobs that respond**
- **Engaging leaders, experts, and peers for jobs, rather than having informational discussions**
- **Wondering how they can have a higher rate of return for their efforts**

For the job seeker, time utilization is critical.

Suggestion: Spend approximately 60% of the time networking and out-reaching (on-line and in-person), 20% with recruiters, and 20% with job boards. Too many job seekers put 90%+ of their effort in applying to positions posted on job boards without much follow-up. They do not take charge of their own destiny.

Serious job seekers must develop a plan, breaking it into smaller steps and making adjustments along the way. The key is to find a path based on passion and commit to it.

> Serious job seekers must develop a plan, breaking it into smaller steps and making adjustments along the way.

Triumph comes with setting practical goals such as achieving a certain number of engagement activities each day including outreach emails, calls, informational meetings, events, web-casts, volunteering, contributing, and follow-up.

Develop a discipline so that day-to-day, week-to-week, month-to-month, these actions become a natural part of the routine. Remember that one opportunity can lead to the next, so create small wins that become the building blocks to opening new doors.

A Job Seeking Warrior recognizes that once they identify their target destination, that even the longest and most challenging job search will be realized by taking one step at a time toward their goal.

“ ”

Power is not given to you, you have to take it.

- Beyoncé Knowles

07: OVERCOMING FEARS AND SETBACKS

Many job seekers have a level of fear, trepidation, or experienced setbacks, which can become big obstacles and slow down the process. Success and failure are part of life.

Career achievements represent an essential sense of identity and self-worth. Overcoming fear of failure, or any uncomfortable situation, is an important challenge for professional and personal growth.

Fear is an emotion that ties into the anticipation of pain or danger. For some, it might be about being too young or old. Too skilled or not qualified enough. Perhaps they are missing a few of the requirements in the job description. Or that they will not stand out over your competition. The obstacle can be real or imagined.

Fear is not always bad; it can provide adrenaline and motivation to help one focus.

Fears derived from rejection, failure, past job history, misunderstandings, and/or going outside one's comfort zone are normal. Between the state of the economy, networking, cold calling, interacting with new people, and interviews, there are many reasons to feel uneasy.

The job seeker can shift their viewpoint by addressing the following.

1. **Do not let your fears or setbacks define you.**
2. **Identify the source of the issue and learn from it.**
3. **Develop positive daily routines and a growth outlook.**
4. **Avoid negative thinking.**
5. **Eat, sleep, and exercise well.**
6. **Engage your network.**

7. **Welcome insights from mentors / coaches / career counselors / peers.**

8. **Take calculated risks and follow instincts.**

9. **Find ways to gain and regain momentum.**

10. **Adjust by starting a new career path and approach.**

11. **View fears and setbacks as a blessing in disguise.**

12. **Put your past behind you and focus on the path forward.**

Every job seeker experiences stress, pressure, and must overcome impediments. Shifting one's outlook can take as much energy as landing a new job.

As Sylvester Stallone said in the Rocky Balboa movie:

> *"You, me, or nobody is gonna hit as hard as life. But it ain't about how hard you hit. It's about how hard you can get hit and keep moving forward; how much you can take and keep moving forward. That's how winning is done!"*

The ability to bounce back quickly, embrace agility, and innovate are important qualities for the job seeker. These attributes take work and do not always come naturally.

Job Seeking Warriors recognize that patience, perseverance, and new perspectives help to overcome fears, setbacks, failures, apprehensions, anxiety, or discomfort to achieve short- and longer-term success.

" "

Doubt is a killer. You just have to know who you are and what you stand for.
- Jennifer Lopez

08: OPTIMIZING SKILLS AND STRENGTHS

Job Seeking Warriors recognize the importance of positioning their skills, education, and work experiences that help them shine when engaging a potential employer.

In this challenging job market, candidates who take the time to develop and know their strengths are in a better position to meet and surpass the needs of an organization and achieve quicker searches.

The days where employers review all submissions manually are long gone. In some cases, applicant tracking systems analyze resumes and curriculum vitae (CVs) to assess the best match using artificial intelligence. Often, intermediaries screen resumes before presenting a short list of candidates to the hiring manager.

Employers take about 20 seconds to review each resume and either drill down further or discard. They screen the cover letter (if applicable), application, online information, and interview for evidence that a candidate possesses the right capabilities.

To pinpoint key attributes:

1. **Identify professional and personal activities you enjoy.**
2. **Reflect on career feedback received along the way.**
3. **Assess skills and strengths that stand out compared to competitors.**
4. **Research why organizations need relevant talents that align to your traits.**
5. **Infuse these qualities in all aspects of the job search from cover letters, resumes, online profiles (e.g., LinkedIn or Xing), and interviews.**
6. **Prepare brief responses and stories around specific situations, responsibilities, activities, and outcomes to anticipated questions highlighting why you are uniquely qualified for the position.**

The Mentor has worked with many job seekers who were extremely qualified for a position, but unless those skills, work experiences, training, additional activities, volunteer work, and education stand out, then the candidate can be passed over.

Taking the time to bring to the forefront these many attributes is key in winning a new position.

Tips to consider:

1. **Review multiple job descriptions to pinpoint key words and expectations.**
2. **When targeting specific companies, review their websites and social posts to identify specific terms, products, services, solutions, and announcements and how they align to your interests.**
3. **Identify "hard skills" related to job requirements and "soft skills" that align to key attributes.**
4. **Assess 10-15 key ("buzz") words to work into resumes, cover letters, and interviews.**
5. **Show how your skills have been demonstrated around specific accomplishments that match with the job description and requirements.**
6. **Ask professional colleagues, mentors, coaches, career counselors, and/or peers for feedback.**

A fellow Mentor once pointed out that candidates will eliminate themselves from contention for a job if they do not have all the skills identified in the job description or interview. It is equally important to remind yourself and potential employers how you can learn, obtain, and develop skills and experience that you may not have at this time. Realize that you can fill in the gaps and rise up in a position that aligns to your career ambitions.

Leveraging these considerations, the job seeker learns the best way to showcase their best qualities throughout the process from the start to finish. Taking one's time and focusing will lead to greater happiness with the selected position and help optimize the job search experience.

Job Seeking Warriors always position their skills and strengths to showcase that they are the best candidate for both posted and hidden positions.

“ ”

It isn't what we say or think that defines us, but what we do.

- Jane Austen

09: CULTIVATING PERSISTENCE

A Job Seeking Warrior realizes that persistence is necessary for success.

Some of the Mentor's best lessons come from setbacks. The job seeker knows that the more they persevere, the more momentum they build, and as a result they will get closer to their aspirations.

When people are determined, we act with conviction. That energy helps connect us in the direction of individuals, groups, organizations, activities, and opportunities in pursuit of our dreams.

There is a famous quote on persistence, *"The race goes not only to the swift, but to those who keep running."*

A job seeker might be qualified, but unless they make the extra effort, they will fall short.

When engaging key contacts and there is no response, do not take it personally; give it some time and follow up. It often takes more than one request to set an action in motion.

The people you are contacting receive hundreds of requests in a day or week. Friendly, professional, follow-up and persuasion centered around value is worthwhile.

Tactful, gentle follow-up emails or phone calls that focus on a company's compelling challenges and how you can contribute impress interviewers, employers, recruiters, experts, leaders, and professionals.

Timing is key. Always be respectful, humble, and organized.

A few ways to develop tenacity:

1. **Take small steps to achieve a sense of accomplishment.**
2. **Avoid lack of activity, growth, or forward movement.**
3. **Stay agile as plans can change.**

4. Try multiple approaches.

5. Develop discipline and strong inner conviction.

6. Practice optimism; regard disappointments as temporary.

7. Cultivate appreciation.

8. Remind yourself of your victories.

9. Write a new career story.

10. Cultivate supporters; bounce ideas off of those you trust.

When the job seeker is dedicated, resilient, and open to new possibilities that appear along the career journey, our ultimate goal will come true.

As an example, one of the Mentor's top mentees scheduled calls/meeting every two or three weeks over a four-month period to review next steps, take notes, and address challenges and obstacles.

Rather than settling for a lesser position, they treated job seeking like training for a marathon race, and in the end obtained a top position that became a springboard for a great career.

When the job seeker is dedicated, resilient, and open to new possibilities that appear along the career journey, our ultimate goal will come true.

The Job Seeking Warrior realizes that persistence is an investment in both the short- and longer-term. Words are not the answer, but rather actions. Each move brings advancement.

“ ”

Perseverance is failing 19 times and succeeding the 20th.

- Julie Andrews Edwards

10: DON'T SETTLE

A friend of the Mentor shared that she had been offered a new job. In hearing about it he realized it was several degrees below her skill and career level. The Mentor asked why she wanted to take it, and she replied, *"Because I'm restless and want to try something new."*

The Mentor suggested that it was best to take a step back and that there were many more great opportunities out there. She responded that she did not have the skills or approach, so it was best to just take the position.

Fortunately, the offer fell through, and she went on to a much better position by putting together a well thought-out, methodical job search that lasted about five months. From this experience, the Mentor realized how ill-equipped many talented people are in charting their own course. Without the right job seeking tools and methodology they not only risk failure to land a job, but also risk settling for a lesser position and potentially less pay.

Many job seekers are tired of the job search, lack confidence, and as a result make the mistake of choosing the first offer, potentially leading to mediocrity. People can get stuck and feel like they don't know how to aspire to a better opportunity. These setbacks can take months or years to fix.

Our level of patience is declining. With the internet and social media, we expect instant gratification. Too many professionals *"settle"* and then become miserable, disheartened, or numb to the exciting opportunities that are in store for them and available in the marketplace.

> Excellence is a place where people who refuse to settle for averageness live; it is where one reaps from all the hard work sown.

Let's face it: change, failure, and taking risks can be distressing. Job seekers sometimes feel that it's easier to settle then to leave their comfort zone. There can be many excuses for complacency, but the Mentor believes it's better to live a life without regrets.

The Job Seeking Warrior must develop a mindset that renews their view of themselves and the marketplace on an ongoing basis. Job seekers must try new approaches and filter out bad habits (or less optimal approaches) from the past that did not work, design a plan of action, and drive it forward.

Excellence is a place where people who refuse to settle for averageness live; it is where one reaps from all the hard work sown. It is a journey of continuous progression toward career goals.

Job Seeking Warriors know it takes time, effort, and patience to find the right position. Get started now. Don't settle.

“ ”

If you haven't found it yet, keep looking. Don't settle. As with all matters of the heart, you'll know when you find it.

- Steve Jobs

CHECKLIST

- [ ] ....

....

- [ ] ....

....

- [ ] ....

....

Chapter Three

POSITIONING FOR TRIUMPH

THE JOB SEEKING WARRIOR'S SKILLSET

1: The Challenge

- Power
- Mission
- Transition
- Job Intelligence
- Crossing Over

2: Developing Strategy

- Begin Now
- Overcome Fears
- Position Strengths
- Persistance
- Don't Settle

3: Positioning for Triumph

- Abundance
- Hidden Opportunities
- Tailor Your Resume
- Plan
- Build Your Brand

4: Proactive Engagement

- Advantage
- Networking
- Fishing
- Cover Letter
- Follow Up

5: Pursuing a Position

- 3-Legged Stool
- Top Economic Descision Maker
- Gatekeeper
- Informational Meeting
- Foot in the Door

6: The Power to Win

- Prepare
- 2-Way Interview
- Salary Negotiation
- Recieve an Offer
- Mentor

11: AN ABUNDANCE OF OPPORTUNITIES

A number of years back, the Mentor sat down for breakfast with a friend and career expert who self-published a book, "Job $ecurity for Life." One of the key messages that she inspired was that there is "an abundance of work" opportunities.

When she shared this idea, the Mentor wondered how it could be true when the job market was so challenging with ups and downs...downsizing and firings...budget cuts...closed doors... and the rest.

She asked him if he ever noticed how many job seekers say or think, "there are no opportunities out there" and yet when you look at company and internet job boards there are many listings.

There are a great number of firms where Human Resources (HR), recruiters, and line of business leaders have visible, open positions and are working hard to fill them. Hidden positions exist and are emerging based on market developments, compelling organizational issues and challenges, as well as word of mouth and referrals.

To further illustrate an abundance of opportunity she asked, *"When you have a job do you ever notice there's so much work that needs to be addressed and often not enough time, expertise, or employees to get it all done?"*

One of the key messages that she inspired was that there is "an abundance of work" opportunities.

She shared that if, for example, you can solve, contribute, or support a large business issue (e.g., worth millions) for the amount of your salary or consulting fee, then the economic decision maker in the organization would consider bringing you on to address the challenge.

Her insights were one of many perspectives the Mentor gained along the way including following trends, listening to leaders, and assessing important business matters that impact increasing revenues, improving operational efficiencies, or cutting costs.

The key is to evaluate how to impact one of these areas along with the realization that all workers need to make a high-quality contribution to be hired, stay employed, as well as increase job security and advancement. The door for getting a new job is never closed.

How often do you hear that one organization is letting one group of employees go and at the same time another department in the same company is hiring? Or that a candidate did not get one position but used their knowledge to get another job in the same firm. Or they didn't get the interview or job and a few months later a new opportunity arises.

> The more the job seeker gets to know what an employer needs, their priorities, how they screen candidates, and make hiring decisions, the greater the likelihood of securing a new position.

The more the job seeker gets to know what an employer needs, their priorities, how they screen candidates, and make hiring decisions, the greater the likelihood of securing a new position.

Years later when the Mentor opened up the author's book, he read the hand-written inscription:

> *"Your creative ingenuity and deep intuition are your job security for life. SHINE ON."*

A Job Seeking Warrior recognizes that the marketplace holds an abundance of opportunities. The key is to keep an open mind, know what you want, expect success, and believe that you deserve victory.

" "

Turn off the tape in your head that tells you there is nothing out there, and make a game out of seeing how many opportunities you can find for yourself and others to whom you might refer a good opportunity.

- Susan E. Race

12: THE HIDDEN JOB MARKET

The hidden job market = the job not posted and/or just emerging.

It is true that there are millions of positions that are never formally posted on job boards or company websites. Many employers choose to save time and money by finding candidates through their own trusted networks or referrals.

Recognize that employers need help. They have problems. There is work that needs to happen beyond the framework of the everyday employees, which becomes an entrance to hidden job opportunities.

The job seeker must think of themselves as an innovator, an entrepreneur, a CEO of their own business.

Participating in the hidden job market requires four practical steps.

1. **Make a list of target companies; do not wait for them to post a job opening.**
    - Identify the priorities, business pain, or compelling issues/challenges you can solve.
    - Assess the trends that impact an organization where investments are being made.
    - Identify contacts in your network, hiring managers, and economic decision makers.
    - Write down a plan of action and commit to a campaign approach for outreach.
    - Subscribe to news alerts (e.g., Google Alerts).
2. **Set up informational meetings with alumni, industry experts, professors, previous employers, peers, hiring managers, and top economic decision makers and their teams.**

- Start engaging by sending an email communicating the identified issue or opportunity in a positive, professional way with alignment to your skills and experiences.
- Join alumni networks and professional organizations and become a contributor.
- Ask trusted contacts to make connections on your behalf.
- Consider short-term and part-time roles as a volunteer, freelancer, contractor, or with a staffing agency to get a foot in the door.
- Assess if more education, training, or experience is helpful.

3. **Brand yourself by updating your social media to reflect your mission.**
    - Update LinkedIn and other online/social media profiles.
    - Market yourself as an expert in your field (e.g., blog, present, volunteer, contribute, etc.).
4. **Spread the word of your search.**

While working in a Fortune 500 company, the Mentor found that budgets were shrinking and advancement was stalled. A former team member who had moved to another Global 500 company identified a hidden position that was emerging on her team. This referral lead to a new position with a big budget and many new challenges.

Another time, the Mentor was coaching a soccer team when a fellow coach referenced a pain point within a large organization that led to a referral to a Senior Vice President and a new consulting position. This lead and foot in the door became a major building block in developing a global consulting business.

In each case, the opportunity was not posted and only through a strong network would the Mentor hear about and act upon a new chapter in his own career journey.

In each case, the opportunity was not posted and only through a strong network would the Mentor hear about and act upon a new chapter in his own career journey.

The hidden job market is constantly changing and on the move. The great hockey player Wayne Gretsky once shared an insight:

> *"I skate to where the puck is going to be, not where it has been."*

Job Seeking Warriors know it takes extra effort to anticipate where opportunities will emerge. They put in the time to engage leaders, their networks, and hiring managers to find hidden job opportunities. They know that even if the job does not appear now, that they'll be at the top of mind for referrals and consideration when a position opens up.

“ ”

There is nothing so far removed from us to be beyond our reach, or so far hidden that we cannot discover it.

- Rene Descartes

13: TAILORING YOUR RESUME

Resumes represent a snapshot of career and educational experiences and play a determining factor on whether the job seeker gets an interview or not.

Today, job applicants need to sway a person or Artificial Intelligence (AI) of their capabilities before they can be recognized for an interview. AI is scanning the resume to look for keywords and phrases in order to identify the candidates best suited for the respective position.

Human Resources (HR), recruiters, and/or hiring managers will review the submission within 20 seconds to assess it for an interview or discard it.

Positioning your resume to show value to a potential employer is what enables it to attract attention. There are many books, articles, posts, and templates on how to write an effective resume. Find examples of resumes that represent successful professionals in your field.

Tailor your resume to the specific job. For example, if they ask for "project management" experience as a key requirement, assess where in your work history you have project management experience and include it.

Characteristics of great resumes include:

- **Applicable expertise that is visible and aligned to the position**
- **Power words that relate to the job description and what the employer values**
- **Quantifiable stats or qualifiable statements to showcase accomplishments**
- **Clean, consistent, and visually pleasing format**

Pay attention to typos, grammar, spacing, formatting, and brevity. Ask one or two friends or colleagues who have professional expertise and are very good writers and/or editors to proof read it.

Make your points brief and to the point. No more than two lines per bulleted item. Consider three to five bullets for each featured work experience, but not too many.

Assess the order of your achievements and the timing of your career. If you are a student or recent graduate, your education will be at the top. Later in your career it will move to the bottom.

Early in a career a one-page resume is the right size; no more than two pages later in one's career.

When writing a resume consider a section called *"Additional Work Experiences"* where you put older or less relevant positions on one line each. For example, if you are getting started in your career you may include building block positions such as waiter/waitress or lifeguard. For job seekers with many years of experience, this approach can consolidate positions and reduce resume size to the benefit of the employer reading it.

Early in a career a one-page resume is the right size; no more than two pages later in one's career.

Include alumni and professional group membership along with any volunteer activities. If you do not have any, make a point to get involved. Employers look for candidates who have experiences outside their school or job.

The Mentor's very successful professional colleague once said, *"I have one master resume and 18 more that I tailor each time depending on the position."*

Job Seeking Warriors continuously refine their resumes to position them in a way that shows value to a specific position of interest. A strong resume plays a key role in the job search to showcase strengths, open doors, increase the interview participation rate, and ultimately win a great new job opportunity.

" "

The challenge of life, I have found, is to build a resume that doesn't simply tell a story about what you want to be, but it's a story of who you want to be.

- Oprah Winfrey

14: PUTTING A PLAN INTO MOTION

Action puts the Job Seeking Warrior on the road to self-confidence and enables small steps forward. When the path forward is opened, energies flow, and tangible rewards are realized.

Putting a strategic plan in place takes effort; however, once in place, it provides the job seeker with a roadmap to become better organized and help achieve success.

For example, all too often job seekers put too much emphasis on just a few activities, such as posting on job boards, which can lead to frustration and lower response rates. It's important to engage in a multi-faceted approach.

Once, a student being mentored shared that they felt like the employers *"held all the cards."* In reality, dedicated job seekers hold many of the cards if they take ownership of the whole end-to-end process.

A major first step of planning is to write it down. A wise person once said, *"A plan not written down is just a dream."*

A few steps to consider:

1. **Take a deep breath, stay calm, and focus.**
2. **Write down career goals that optimize your skills, experiences, strengths, and passions.**
3. **Identify and research ideal companies of interest including top leaders and influential contacts.**
4. **Build a to-do list for key job search next steps.**
5. **Develop your personal brand.**
6. **Engage in networking opportunities.**
7. **Schedule informational meetings.**

Develop and maintain a spreadsheet tracking your progress from start to finish. Set quantifiable goals for each day, week, and month. Share updates with a trusted, supportive friend or career coach.

Company Contact	Email Sent	Phone	Scheduled Call	Informational Meeting	Interview	Comments / Next Steps	Opportunity Identified	Offer Recieved	Confirmed
Company A	X	X	X	X					
Company B	X	X	X	X	X	X	X	X	X
Company C	X	X	X	X					

Give your plan time to materialize. Stay consistent, persistent, and practice patience. Plant seeds that will take hold and grow along the way.

> Give your plan time to materialize. Stay consistent, persistent, and practice patience. Plants seeds that will take hold and grow along the way.

As an analogy, consider how opening up a safe or a lock is similar to opening up a job opportunity. Turning the dial just one time will not open it. Each turn of the dial left or right is an advance that eventually leads to it opening, or from a job seeker's perspective: opening up new opportunities.

A colleague once remarked, *"Taking small steps is like banging on a rock with another very hard rock; it won't break right away, but if you keep banging eventually it will break. Never give up."*

Job Seeking Warriors recognize that putting a plan in motion makes the process of finding an excellent job less intimidating, more organized, and more enjoyable.

"

The backbone of success is …hard work, determination, good planning and perseverance.

- Mia Hamm

15: BUILDING YOUR BRAND

The Job Seeking Warrior realizes that developing their own professional brand helps improve the conversion rate on offers. It's important to differentiate from other candidates who are competing for the same jobs.

Developing a brand sounds challenging. It can be viewed as an activity for someone else (e.g., C-suite executives, top leaders) or perhaps unnecessary, but it supports building credibility in your field.

A professional brand signals to a potential employer more about you by highlighting your strengths, growing your reputation, building trust, and showcasing your unique talents.

A few tips on ways to build your brand:

1. **Pinpoint the skills, expertise, and interests that you want to share.**
2. **Assess your audience.**
3. **Learn more about other leaders and experts in your desired field or industry.**
4. **Update your social media profiles (e.g., LinkedIn, Twitter) including using a professional photo.**
5. **Ask for recommendations (e.g., LinkedIn).**
6. **Grow your online presence (professional tweets, posts, blogs, articles, etc.).**
7. **Network and engage with university alumni and professional groups.**
8. **Assess opportunities to participate in an organization and showcase your skills.**
9. **Request informational meetings to both learn and show more visibility with organizations of interest and within your chosen field.**
10. **Practice helping others and giving back.**
11. **Consider your own professional website (WordPress, GoDaddy, Site Building Tools).**

Your professional brand will help you shine. Remember to always be authentic to who you are and what you want to communicate.

Once you lay the groundwork you will be in a better position to realize the benefits, but like anything else it takes time and dedication. Set ongoing goals and pay attention to how your audience responds.

The messages you share, combined with your daily interactions, define your evolving professional brand. As you connect with different individuals and new networks, your brand will grow.

Often an employer's observations and decision-making process are shaped without the candidate knowing. For example, a potential employer may check online information or reach out to their own network to find out more about a candidate in preparing for an interview or making a hiring decision.

> Your professional brand will help you shine. Remember to always be authentic to who you are and what you want to communicate.

Positive attention by the job seeker to their brand helps align their strengths and interests to their desired position. Even a small amount of branding can make a big difference. Focus on quality rather than the quantity of branding endeavors.

Job Seeking Warriors develop a professional brand to establish themselves as leaders, experts, and/or quality contributors, and to help open doors and create new opportunities.

" "

Branding demands commitment; commitment to continual re-invention; striking chords with people to stir their emotions; and commitment to imagination.

- Sir Richard Branson

CHECKLIST

- [ ] ....

....

- [ ] ....

....

- [ ] ....

....

Chapter Four

PROACTIVE ENGAGEMENT

THE JOB SEEKING WARRIOR'S SKILLSET

1: The Challenge

Power

Mission

Transition

Job Intelligence

Crossing Over

2: Developing Strategy

Begin Now

Overcome Fears

Position Strengths

Persistance

Don't Settle

3: Positioning for Triumph

Abundance

Hidden Opportunities

Tailor Your Resume

Plan

Build Your Brand

4: Proactive Engagement

Advantage

Networking

Fishing

Cover Letter

Follow Up

5: Pursuing a Position

3-Legged Stool

Top Economic Descision Maker

Gatekeeper

Informational Meeting

Foot in the Door

6: The Power to Win

Prepare

2-Way Interview

Salary Negotiation

Recieve an Offer

Mentor

16: GAINING THE INFORMATION ADVANTAGE

Job Seeking Warriors obtain an information advantage during each step of the journey.

They put in the extra effort to acquire unique knowledge by gaining first-hand and researched insights, which is very useful during informational meetings, interviews, and follow-up.

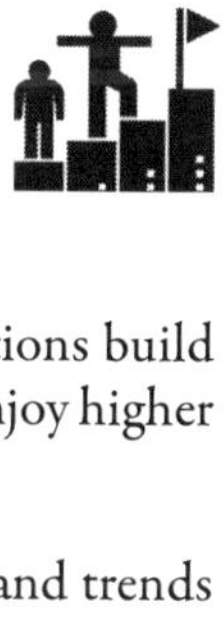

Yet many job seekers do not take the time to acquire readily available key data points. They overlook leveraging alumni and professional networks and online resources to learn more about their target organizations, top leaders, and hiring managers.

Those who view information as a valuable resource in preparing for key interactions build momentum, experience fewer surprises, respond faster and more accurately, and enjoy higher rates of return.

They look for both posted and hidden jobs based on compelling business issues and trends such as:

- **Plans for revenues and growth**
- **New innovations and trends**
- **Updates in regulations, compliance, and safety**
- **Mergers and acquisitions**
- **Improvements to customer care**
- **Inefficiencies impacting people, processes, technology, or data**
- **Opportunities to reduce costs and risks**

Successful candidates make the effort to gather information by investigating, exploring, asking questions, listening, and learning.

Key techniques to gain knowledge include:

- ➡ **Holistic approach - View information in context of the big picture**
- ➡ **Speed - Ability to obtain and leverage public data quickly**
- ➡ **Analysis - Identify trends and pain points of an organization**
- ➡ **Research - Acquire and analyze alerts, announcements, and social media**
- ➡ **Role-based knowledge - Gather information specific to a position**
- ➡ **First-hand knowledge - Outreach to contacts to understand a situation**

Job seekers who anticipate the power of information will be in better control of job-related interactions.

Tangible steps forward include:

1. **Researching target organizations and potential positions.**
2. **Going online and evaluating a variety of dream job descriptions.**
3. **Engaging with organizations that warrant a 3-pronged campaign approach:**
    - Identifying contacts you know directly or in your network (e.g., university alumni)
    - Sharing your job credentials by posting, reaching out to a recruiter, or utilizing a line of business contact
    - Confirming and engaging the economic decision makers and their teams
4. **Participating in alumni and professional networks.**
5. **Seeking informational meetings and discussions.**

Job seekers who pay careful attention acquiring pertinent information will experience a competitive advantage over the many candidates who seek the same position.

As an employer himself, the Mentor sees very clearly when applicants have taken the time to do their research and gain an information advantage. If a top candidate puts in the effort they will stand out and can rise up to win the position.

The great tennis player Arthur Ashe once said, *"One important key to success is self-confidence. An important key to self-confidence is preparation."*

Job Seeking Warriors make sense of the information at a marketplace, organization, and individual level to achieve more successful outcomes and reach their full potential.

“ ”

Knowledge is power.

\- Francis Bacon

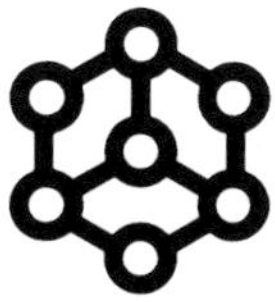

17: ALUMNI AND PROFESSIONAL NETWORKS

Job Seeking Warriors realize that networking is one of the most valuable resources available during their career journey.

The job search has much higher returns when the individual makes purposeful connections and broadens their horizons. Alumni and professional networks, nonprofits, and charities are all great places to provide support and connect to new opportunities.

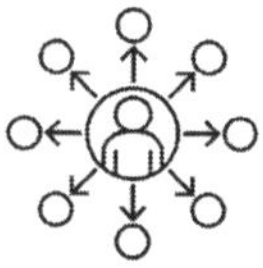

While many are aware of the value of making meaningful contacts as a concept, only a subset of the candidates has scratched the surface to fully appreciate the many benefits. This realization goes beyond just showing up at a meeting or joining an online group as a passive participant.

The Job Seeking Warrior understands that the best rewards are achieved when contributing to the group. Good things come to those who put in their time, energy, and effort to a small or greater degree over a sustained amount of time. While short-term participation is good; having a longer-term outlook to contribute provides greater returns.

When connecting to a network group consider the following:

1. **Identify and assess if the group is right for you.**
    - Attend professional events, webinars, meet-ups, workshops, and conferences.
    - Join select online groups (e.g., LinkedIn, Facebook). Contact the group leaders and active participants to learn more.
    - Assess which special interest groups or committees interest you.

2. **Engage, participate, and volunteer in your selected group.**
    - Set small practical goals to get started or advance further as a participant.

- Help other members in the group based on their needs.
- Showcase the skills that are important to your next job by volunteering.
- When between jobs, participate to fill gaps of employment.
- Find ways to provide support and give back.

3. **Reach out to fellow alumni, leaders, professionals, professors, experts, and hiring managers for informational meetings.**

Assess a realistic amount of time that you can participate in the network (e.g., number of hours per week or month) and prioritize it as part of your routine. Focus on building relationships and providing value. Assess what commitments you can make for the better good of the group and follow up on them.

For the Mentor, networking works best when putting in the time to have a longer-term versus short-term view. Identifying one or a small set of priority projects at a given time works best. Finding the best way to lead or contribute is important; it is not enough to merely show up to a meeting or event.

Developing a positive network experience can lead to referrals, informational insights, recharged energy, recognition, and most importantly great satisfaction as a team player.

Demonstrating on a resume and in action that you can provide a significant level of time, expertise, and/or support helps the job seeker stand out.

Developing a positive network experience can lead to referrals, informational insights, recharged energy, recognition, and most importantly great satisfaction as a team player.

Job Seeking Warriors are more likely to learn about job openings and surface hidden opportunities when they proactively participate in high-quality networks.

“ ”

The richest people in the world look for and build networks, everyone else looks for work.

- Robert T. Kiyosaki

18: HOW MANY RODS TO CATCH ONE FISH?

The Job Seeking Warrior understands both the need to engage a significant quantity of organizations and individuals (aka *"the numbers game"*) and the importance of a strong, high-quality performance during a job search campaign.

Working on and refining job seeking skills improves results. Relying on luck or an opportunity simply falling in your lap is risky.

Job Seeking Warriors put a plan in motion to reach out to *"X"* number of organizations and key contacts to open doors. They focus on quality discussions, build relationships, communicate their unique value, address pain points, and develop positive impressions that lead to more *"yes"* responses, referrals, and scheduled next steps.

Ask the following questions.

- **How many organizations do you reach out to each week or month?**
- **How many are with job boards, HR or talent recruiters, your network, or top decision makers, leaders, or their teams?**
- **How many result in a scheduled next step or referral?**

Consider when you encounter a low number of responses:

- **You are not connecting to enough quality contacts to achieve your goals.**
- **Both posted and hidden job opportunities exist but are not being addressed by way of outreach, engagement, and referrals.**

Take a close look in the mirror to assess your job seeking efforts. If you feel you can do more but are frustrated, step back and calmly evaluate the situation. Identify one obstacle at a time to overcome. Ask a trusted mentor, coach, guidance council, professional, peer, or friend for suggestions.

Continuously monitor your progress. Write down, track, and measure your activities. Strive for continuous improvement, understanding, and adjustments to your approach. What may have worked in one situation might need to be modified in another situation. Stay agile.

Always remember that you can shift your own attitude and must adapt to the mindset of the prospective employers and contacts. Stay positive.

The Mentor's sales friend once said, *"Winning a deal is like fishing. In order to catch one fish, you need to have many rods in the water."*

If you fish in water with too few fish, the chance of catching a fish is small, and/or it might take a long time. The key is to target opportunities with a focused 3-pronged approach and develop a strategic, systematic, and disciplined plan of action.

Always remember that you can shift your own attitude and must adapt to the mindset of the prospective employers and contacts. Stay positive.

For example, over a week's time it is better to engage three to five excellent contacts or organizations with a plan of follow-up in one to three days, then to reach out to 20 by way of a job board in one week with minimal follow-up. Build momentum.

Persistent small steps on a daily, weekly, and monthly basis will bring you closer to your next job. Celebrate small successes along the way.

The Job Seeking Warrior takes control of their job and career journey by multiplying the number of opportunities and reflecting that every day is a new day. Make the most of it.

" "

You miss 100% of the shots you don't take.

- Wayne Gretzky

19: THE COVER LETTER

A compelling cover letter (or email) introduces the Job Seeking Warrior as the top candidate for a position based on their skills, education, and work experiences that provide value to the target organization.

It is important to identify and research the person to whom you are writing the letter based on their role, organization, trends, and customer base. The goal is to get a response and turn it into an appointment either by phone, face-to-face, or a referral, resulting in an informational meeting or interview.

Elements of the letter:

1. **Start with a "subject" that focuses on value or a relevant point derived from your investigation or connection to the opportunity with the first words, such as "Please Review" or "Introduction."**
2. **Craft a brief opening paragraph that aligns to the theme of your subject and ties to the benefits that you can deliver based on their requirements or potential needs.**
3. **Next use bullets (vs. long paragraphs) showing areas of interest to the recipient by bridging your strengths to what the potential employer values.**

   Example supporting topics on how you led or supported:
   - Increasing revenues and growth
   - Improving operational efficiencies or employee performance
   - Reducing costs
   - Supporting customers, partners, or suppliers
   - Addressing a compelling issue, challenge or opportunity
   - Assessing immediate results with a longer-term view

   Note: Where possible quantify the measurable results and use the language from the job description or based on your research.

4. **Develop a closing paragraph with a "call to action" with an "either/or" approach versus "yes/no" such as, "Which time works better to connect, Tuesday morning at 10 AM or Thursday at 1:30 PM?"**

Sometimes this letter goes directly to the identified professional, or if they are senior enough, they may have an executive assistant (or team member). In this case, the letter should be addressed to both, but emailed to the associate if you only have their email address with a request to forward it. Also, it is ideal if you have a contact who can forward it for you as a way of introduction.

Too often cover letters are more about the *"I"* vs. the *"WIITFM"* (What's In It For Me) from the recipient's view. Keep this letter brief (e.g., up to one page), to-the-point, and where possible link to an interesting and relevant article, press release, or social media post from the view point of the employer.

It's important to consider that the resume may or may not be included, sometimes it's best to gain interest first, and then send it as a follow-up.

Once the letter is sent, if you have not heard back, commit to following up within a reasonable amount of time (i.e., one to three days). Of course, the best scenario occurs when they quickly respond and actively engage in an appointment or next step.

The Mentor has written thousands of cover letters and coached many candidates on how to do it. Taking the time to deploy this best practice, when appropriate, is the equivalent of sending an arrow from a bow with the goal to reach the right mark.

Focusing on high priority topics that the employer values helps a candidate stand out.

When the Job Seeking Warrior takes the time to engage prospective employers with a repeatable outreach methodology that they can use throughout their career, they will continuously learn, and they will experience a higher rate of success.

“ ”

Let me warn you once again that this is going to be a letter unlike any you have written. It will only be one page long, but it will require more care, patience, and consistent effort than any other business correspondence you've ever written.

- Anthony Parinello, Selling to VITO (Very Important Top Officer)

20: THE FOLLOW-UP CALL

The Job Seeking Warrior recognizes that they must follow-up engagement activities by contacting key individuals. The goal is to zero in on opportunities by scheduling informational meetings, interviews, or getting referrals.

While many job seekers rely on posting resumes on job boards, sending emails, and waiting for responses, the proactive approach of making a follow-up call (or sending a brief, friendly follow-up email) and scheduling next steps is the best way to proceed, especially when the initial outreach has not resulted in a response.

When reaching out it is best to display a confident, positive, and humble attitude; give it your best each and every time.

Steps to consider include:

1. **Before making contact:**
    - Look up the key contact on LinkedIn or other social channels or internet sites.
    - Write down a few notes based on research about them, their organization, and recent posts or announcements.
2. **Upon making the call:**
    - Say their name. Thank them for their time.
    - Reference the email that you already sent by way of the date and compelling topic.
    - Quickly reference a common contact (i.e., referral), network, announcement, or point.
    - Briefly frame up the goal of the call and the value you bring based on specific points related to their requirements, compelling business issues or challenges, and how you can contribute.

3. **Confirm the next step:**

    - The ending statement of the call should suggest a next step such as an informational meeting, interview, referral to a team member, colleague, or other professional.
        - Frame it as an "either/or" statement versus a "yes or no" such as "would it be better to schedule time next Tuesday AM or Thursday PM for 30 minutes?" versus "can we follow up?"
    - Send a follow-up confirmation such as a meeting invitation and a brief summary note.

Follow-up calls should be quick and concise. Keep in mind you have 20 seconds to make an exceptional first impression. Save the longer conversation for a scheduled meeting date and time (i.e., 30 minutes).

During this time, ensure you have a quality work environment. Clear your desk. Enter the outcome on your tracking sheet (e.g., spoke with, left message, or spoke to a colleague, etc.).

Practice your approach with a professional friend, mentor, or coach. Recognize that outreach does not work every time. Guard against an *"all"* or *"nothing"* mentality.

The Mentor suggests that job seekers follow their initial contact with a friendly, professional call within one to three days to let the key contact know to look for the email.

A good pretense is that you are "checking in" and perhaps have found a new piece of information of interest (i.e. article, blog, post, thought leadership, news, announcement, etc.).

If there is zero response from the follow-up email, then call the organization and ask to be directed to the individual or their team member or assistant. A brief, friendly call or voicemail works very well such as...

> *Hello << First Name >>. This is << Name >>. I sent you an email with the subject "XYZ" on <date/time> requesting an informational meeting to explore and learn more from your journey and insights. I referenced a recent << news item, press release, announcement, compelling business issue, or trend >> that I would appreciate learning more about from a career standpoint. Thanks for your consideration and reply. My contact information is on the email or please call << cell number >>.*

If a door opens be happy and grateful. If not, move on and keep trying.

Job Seeking Warriors make the extra effort by following up. This approach leads to more opportunities, more interviews, and a better chance of finding a job faster.

Diligent follow-up and follow-through will set you apart from the crowd and communicate excellence.

- John C. Maxwell

CHECKLIST

- [ ] ....

  ....

- [ ] ....

  ....

- [ ] ....

  ....

Chapter Five

PURSUING A POSITION

THE JOB SEEKING WARRIOR'S SKILLSET

1: The Challenge

Power | Mission | Transition | Job Intelligence | Crossing Over

2: Developing Strategy

Begin Now | Overcome Fears | Position Strengths | Persistance | Don't Settle

3: Positioning for Triumph

Abundance | Hidden Opportunities | Tailor Your Resume | Plan | Build Your Brand

4: Proactive Engagement

Advantage | Networking | Fishing | Cover Letter | Follow Up

5: Pursuing a Position

3-Legged Stool | Top Economic Descision Maker | Gatekeeper | Informational Meeting | Foot in the Door

6: The Power to Win

Prepare | 2-Way Interview | Salary Negotiation | Recieve an Offer | Mentor

21: THE 3-PRONGED CAMPAIGN APPROACH

The Mentor often asks how the job seeker is engaging potential employers' organizations. Many times, the answer is by simply posting on a job board, company's website, or perhaps sending a resume to HR or an organization's recruiter. The next question is how many positions has the job seeker applied for in the last 30 to 60 days. The answer is often *"many!"* Clearly, the job seeker is not receiving the response they desire.

The 3-pronged campaign is a time-tested, proven approach to increasing response rate centered around:

1. **Finding excellent opportunities**
2. **Assessing who you know**
3. **Identifying the economic decision maker**

Once an organization rises to the level of high interest, then the Job Seeking Warrior should take the time to fully engage to increase knowledge, build momentum, identify opportunities, and gain traction to win a job.

For example, consider a 3-legged stool, if one or two legs are in place but not the third, the whole structure falls down. In the same way, a Job Seeking Warrior should pursue all three of the following in a professional, assertive, respectful, and positive way:

1. **Find excellent opportunities**
    - Evaluate posted and hidden opportunities in the respective company. Recognize compelling events such as market trends, growth, new products or services, or a merger and acquisition.
    - If you see a position posted, research it to assess why it was posted. Understand what prompted the employer to make investments in this position. Follow the money and emerging priorities. Post or send your resume to be considered for an interview.

2. **Assess who you know**
    - Check with your network. Do a search on a platform or app such as LinkedIn, Xing, or the equivalent. Engage with your network to request informational meetings. Reach out to a fellow alumnus you know (or don't know) who can share insights.

3. **Who is the economic decision maker?**
    - Find out who is the top leader for the position you're going after. Is it a CEO, CXO, president, or a line of business lead such as the head of sales, marketing, finance, operations, HR, Customer Service, etc.? Reach out to them or one of their team members.

The overall goal is to...

1. **Look for ways to share relevant company news, announcements, and activities that connect to your strengths and interests (reference in cover letters, conversations, follow-up emails).**
2. **Confirm face-to-face or phone call meetings (up to 30 minutes).**
3. **Learn more about the organization, make contacts, and request any referrals.**
4. **Pinpoint opportunities that lead to interviews and job.**
5. **Increase your visibility (and brand) by showing you are executing positive, professional due diligence.**

The Mentor has witnessed how using this method turns the job seeker's search into a purposeful campaign centered around proactive engagement. It helps them gain knowledge, confidence, and build a network. This approach can send a signal to a potential employer that the candidate is interested and focused. When practiced in a positive, professional way, it can help identify posted and hidden opportunities.

> This approach can send a signal to a potential employer that the candidate is interested and focused.

Job Seeking Warriors maintain and prioritize a group of target companies and individuals. This list remains dynamic as organizations can be added, subtracted, or moved due to changing priorities. One position may close and another open, so continuously engaging in a friendly, focused manner is an important key to success.

“ ”

For leaders [or job seekers] to be effective, they need to connect with people.

- John C. Maxwell

22: WHO IS THE TOP ECONOMIC DECISION MAKER?

The Job Seeking Warrior is always aware of the top person with the ultimate power to say *"yes"* or *"no"* to hiring a candidate. These economic decision makers are interested to know what a job candidate can contribute to impact and add value to the entire organization.

Top leaders are interested in the overall success of the organization, staying ahead of competitors, and achieving tangible, measurable results. They care about one or more of the universal business actualities.

1. **Increasing revenues and growth**
2. **Improving operational efficiencies and effectiveness**
3. **Ongoing cost cutting to increase margins**

Whether interviewing with the top leader or their team, the job seeker must always position their skills, education, and work experiences to fit the leader's requirements.

Leaders personify one or more of the following characteristics.

- **Vision**
- **Passion**
- **Holistic outlook**
- **Decisiveness**
- **Continuously assessing trends and innovation**
- **Power**
- **Authenticity**
- **Resiliency**
- **Ability to assess new ideas**
- **Consideration to take risks and lower them**
- **Ability to exceed expectations with customers, employees, partners, and stakeholders**

When interacting with top leaders, it is essential to demonstrates confidence, energy, and an unlimited interest to succeed based on positioning specific values that align to the organization and their goals.

Key considerations include:

1. **Identifying and researching top leaders who have various functions such as:**
    - CEO or President
    - CXO or head of a line of business
    - Owner or Partner
    - Senior or Executive VP

2. **Assessing if the top economic decision maker has an assistant or key team member who can help you gain access and/or provide insights.**
    - Spot gatekeepers who are blocking access to the top leaders.
    - Interviewing with team members is helpful, but realize they often need to get the confirmation from the top leader to finalize a hiring decision.

3. **Keeping in mind that being diverted to human resources (HR) is not necessarily a dead-end.**
    - If the top leader refers you to HR or a recruiter in a thoughtful way, it can represent a next step to schedule a quality interview and gain traction.

Connecting with top economic leaders may feel uncomfortable at first, but if you apply a strong sense of determination and purpose you will achieve greater success and satisfaction in your career. Think of them as peers who have gone further and often longer in their journey regardless of their age.

The Mentor has found that either direct engagement with the economic decision maker(s), or indirect by a colleague on the team who advocates for the candidate, represents a very important part of the process. After all, until an offer is made and confirmed, the job cannot be obtained and finalized.

Job Seeking Warriors focus on ways to engage top leaders by communicating how they can provide tangible value, positioning themselves as indispensable, and demonstrating a results-oriented focus.

“ ”

Interviews and hiring decisions connect to a top economic decision maker who looks for contributions to their organization, and the impact to internal or external stakeholders.

\- Richard D. Blumberg

23: GETTING PAST THE GATEKEEPERS

How often does a job seeker reach a decision-maker or key team member on the first call or email? For most candidates, the chances of a first time, cursory response is incredibly low.

Frequently the first connection is with a talent recruiter, executive assistant, team member, office administrator, or a human resources video interview. They are the real or perceived gatekeepers and play a key part in the outcome of getting a meeting, interview, or identifying an opportunity.

Gatekeepers play an important role in an organization to protect decision makers' and hiring managers' time by screening applicants and turning away those whose requests are considered unimportant.

For job seekers engaging gatekeepers with emails and calls, perhaps getting rejected or ignored, can be frustrating. Every year a company can receive hundreds or thousands of responses for posted (and hidden) positions. For that reason, if a top leader or team member recommends a job candidate, it can help move their credentials toward the top of the pile and past the gatekeeper.

The key is to stop thinking of gatekeepers as obstacles, but rather as valued members of the organization who will consider the job seeker's request if they see the value, are treated with respect, and that the request brings low perceived risks or distractions.

Techniques to master include:

1. **Identifying the right contacts through research:**
    - Tap your alumni, professional, friends, and family network.
    - Aim high by focusing on the top decision makers and their teams.
    - Confirm the top leader's executive assistant or team member's contact information.
    - Verify emails or, at a minimum, the main office phone number.

2. **Drill down into the company website, social media, LinkedIn, and internet searches.**
   - Push outside your comfort zone and get creative.
   - Point out a challenge or problem burdening the company per your research.
   - After sending cover letters or emails, make follow-up phone calls.

3. **Engage the gatekeeper as a valued resource.**
   - Befriend them by building repour, listening, and omitting small talk.
   - Clearly frame up your objective by leading with value and suggested next steps.
   - Manage any objections thoughtfully and succinctly.
   - Assess if the gatekeep has the power to set up the meeting on behalf of the top leader.
   - Include the gatekeeper on the follow-up email (as appropriate).

4. **Know when to move on, and either give it a rest or try other contacts.**

The Mentor routinely suggests turning a gatekeeper into an ally. When possible find out about them by way of quick research (e.g., LinkedIn, Xing). It's important to be brief and authentic. Engage them by email or phone. Keep the message simple and make it easy for them to say *"Yes!"*

Once the gatekeeper buys into your vision and goals with a positive engagement, they are more likely to pass you along to the top economic decision maker, hiring manager, and their teams. Celebrate and track each success, and when there has been meaningful dialogue, send a thank you email.

It is important for a Job Seeking Warrior to embrace the gatekeeper, recognize their value, view them as an advocate to gain access to top leaders or team members, and move their job agenda forward.

“ ”

Definition of gatekeeper:
1: one that tends or guards a gate.
2: a person who controls access.

- Merriam-Webster Dictionary

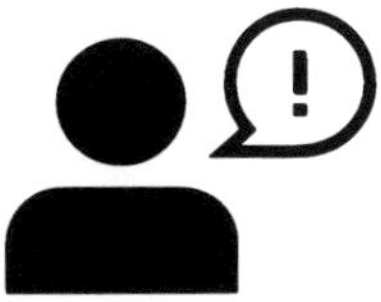

24: THE INFORMATIONAL MEETING'S IMPORTANCE

The Job Seeking Warrior targets specific companies as potential employers and identifies key individuals in those organizations and/or in the respective field as informed advisors.

They know that the best way to gain insights and increase visibility is to engage in informational discussions. These meetings are derived from referrals, leveraging a network, or at times from cold calls.

Informational discussions have many benefits.

- Investigating your initial ideas and providing advice on career options
- Gathering first-hand information on the company or field
- Gaining tips on how to take the next steps and lessons learned
- Developing relationships and a team of advocates to alert you when opportunities arise
- Growing your brand, building momentum, and boosting confidence

Some job seekers are uncomfortable reaching out to new contacts, but keep in mind that many professionals enjoy sharing their journey and giving back.

6 steps for securing informational meetings:

1. Identify people in organizations of interest; engage them by way of emails, follow-up calls, and social media outreach in a polite, professional way.
2. Secure meetings by asking your network for referrals to successful individuals in target organizations, or in your field of interest, to gain career insights.
3. Keep the meeting brief (up to 30 minutes is typical, 60 minutes if appropriate).

- Do your homework by way of research and writing down thoughtful questions.
- Succinctly frame up your background and goals.

4. **Suggest scheduling a follow-up meeting versus a one-off discussion.**
5. **Send a thank you note.**
6. **Follow up to share progress. Include a link to a relevant article, blog, or social media post.**

Treat the informational meeting as a professional discussion and conduct yourself accordingly. If you are weighing several types of jobs or career options, use this approach to gather more knowledge about each one.

Example questions to ask during an informational meeting:

- ➡ **How did you get into this position from your university to now?**
- ➡ **What are one or two examples of priorities you are working on now?**
- ➡ **What do you enjoy the most about your role and company?**
- ➡ **What trends are driving your field, company, industry?**
- ➡ **Write down specific questions based on your research.**

Upon reflection, the Mentor finds that the best candidates leverage the informational meeting with patience and a genuine interest to learn and assess next steps.

Job seekers commit a tactical error when they primarily speak about wanting a job (especially when none may exist), and embrace less the process of finding a job.

When a job interview is secured, where possible, it is very positive to engage in an informational meeting with someone in the organization or who has perspective on it such as a supplier, partner or customer, to learn more about the organization and/or role. Taking the initiative to seek out more insights, shows the potential employer that the candidate is interested, and the information found can help formulate interview questions, knowledge, and confidence.

By making connections and engaging successful professionals, the Job Seeking Warrior sets the stage for making advancements, learning about new or hidden opportunities, standing out when interviews take place, and increasing the odds of success when hiring decisions occur.

“ ”

We meet the people we're supposed to when the time is just right.

- Alyson Noel

25: A FOOT IN THE DOOR

Many job seekers set their sights on a full-time employee position with benefits, which is a great objective, and overlook other opportunities to get a foot in the door. Landing a position can be challenging, but there is more than one way to navigate toward a high-quality job.

Job Seeking Warriors consider all options to achieve their goals at the target company including:

- **Working a part-time job**
- **Seeking a temporary, contract, freelance, intern, or consulting position**
- **Taking a job with a partner organization in the desired company's ecosystem**
- **Volunteering to support a project or initiative with a nonprofit or charity**

Whether in school or between jobs, remember part-time work can represent a means to an end. Job seekers can dramatically increase their chances of landing a full-time position when they are working.

A 15- to 25-hour-per-week job, even at lower pay or minimum wage, may not seem ideal, but perspective employers will respect that you are working in a position relevant to your career ambitions.

A temporary or contract position can also help get a foot in the door with a desired organization. Working in one of these roles can lead to networking from the inside and showcasing your skills and achievements to hiring individual(s). In addition, some job seekers will identify a small consulting project and get paid to provide deliverables around a scope of work. In either scenario, a job seeker can get paid while gaining visibility.

Employment gaps can represent a "red flag" to employers that you are on the sidelines, a less desirable worker, and/or not putting forth the effort to utilize your time in the best way. Considering all options to gain a foothold can provide a stepping-stone into a quality organization and position.

For example, the Mentor had one colleague who desired working for a top high-tech software manufacturing organization. Despite many interviews and rejections, he would end up with a smaller, lesser known partner organization in the same ecosystem. After several years, and on the third try, he was finally hired by the desired company. By building up his work experiences, he easily became the candidate of choice when an opportunity finally surfaced.

Another job seeker's approach is to volunteer at a university, trade organization, or charity that is relevant to target organizations. They assess supporting a mini-project with a leader, expert, group that adds value in the short-term and is based on reasonably small number of hours per week or month. The goal is to interact and showcase skills, build the professional brand, and contribute.

The goal is to interact and showcase skills, build the professional brand, and contribute.

Nonprofit organizations need help and welcome volunteer support. This technique can enhance existing talents and work experiences and develop new ones. The barrier of entry when donating time is low, while the benefits of volunteerism are very high. The short-term gains are incredibly positive, and the long-term value of your contribution will last a lifetime.

Job Seeking Warriors are innovative, creative, agile, and open to various forms of work to get a foot in the door. Given the opportunity, they will prove themselves and identify many new opportunities.

“ ”

In business it is most often all about getting your foot in the door and once you do, everything opens up and things start to naturally progress into bigger and more opportunities.

- Lori Greiner

CHECKLIST

- [ ] ....

....

- [ ] ....

....

- [ ] ....

....

Chapter Six

THE POWER TO WIN

THE JOB SEEKING WARRIOR'S SKILLSET

1: The Challenge

- Power
- Mission
- Transition
- Job Intelligence
- Crossing Over

2: Developing Strategy

- Begin Now
- Overcome Fears
- Position Strengths
- Persistance
- Don't Settle

3: Positioning for Triumph

- Abundance
- Hidden Opportunities
- Tailor Your Resume
- Plan
- Build Your Brand

4: Proactive Engagement

- Advantage
- Networking
- Fishing
- Cover Letter
- Follow Up

5: Pursuing a Position

- 3-Legged Stool
- Top Economic Descision Maker
- Gatekeeper
- Informational Meeting
- Foot in the Door

6: The Power to Win

- Prepare
- 2-Way Interview
- Salary Negotiation
- Recieve an Offer
- Mentor

26: INTERVIEW PREPARATION

The Job Seeking Warrior knows that landing a quality interview with a prime organization is a great accomplishment. They know that if they want to win the job, they must be ready.

For many interviewers, a lack of thoughtful questions from the candidate can be a showstopper. Take the time to write down questions based on your research to show the reasons you are the best candidate for the position, and did your homework.

Preparing for an interview means making a commitment to give it your all by considering how your goals and experiences align to the position, and why the employer is hiring.

Use the job description as a key indicator. Take your time with it. This write-up will provide hints of what the employer will ask during the interview and expectations. Align your skills, education, and work experiences to show you are highly qualified. Create an outline mapping out the position point-by-point to your strengths.

Plan to put in the time to learn about a range of information addressing the organization's mission, job roles, products/services, ecosystem/partners, industry(s), leaders, news, culture, brief history, compelling trends, issues, and competition.

Research the career background of the individual(s) who will interview you, their line of business (or department), and if possible, their organization's leadership.

When there are multiple interviewers, prepare questions to ask based on their role (e.g., an engineer would receive different questions then a sales or finance leader).

Taking time to learn more so that you come across as a knowledgeable candidate is essential. The amount of time can vary from a little to a great deal, but zero time preparing will be evident very quickly. A further motivation to prepare is to gain a competitive advantage over other candidates.

Top considerations:

1. **Commit to studying for the interview like it is an exam or at least a quiz.**
2. **Review the job description in detail and break it down into smaller parts.**
3. **Prepare for questions based on the job description and research that highlight your strengths.**
4. **Evaluate the organization to decide if it's a good fit for your career interests.**
5. **Plan for different types of interviews (e.g., phone, video conference, first, second, third round).**
6. **Practice a mock interview with a friend or professional (e.g., career counselor or mentor/coach).**
7. **Anticipate what will go into a "Thank You" email, and send it within 24 hours of the interview.**

There are many sources for gaining insights. Between informational meetings, alumni and professional networks, organizations' websites, social medial channels (Twitter, LinkedIn, etc.), and the internet, there is a wealth of information to be found on the organization, interviewer(s), and the desired position.

If possible, try to connect with someone in the organization or industry who has roughly the same role or who had a similar position in their career. Learn from their experiences and expertise.

In the Mentor's experience, once the top candidates are confirmed for an interview, they each have a chance to win the position. However, the ones who are most prepared will stand out and elevate themselves during the interview process. Too often multiple applicants share similar credentials, but the one who takes the time to get ready has a better chance to succeed.

If possible, try to connect with someone in the organization or industry who has roughly the same role or who had a similar position in their career.

Job Seeking Warriors prioritize preparation for each interview throughout their career to continuously learn, build confidence, and increase the odds of winning the position over their competition.

“”

Preparation, I have often said, is rightly two-thirds of any venture.

- Amelia Earhart

27: THE 2-WAY INTERVIEW

Interviewing is a two-way street for both the employer and candidate to assess if there is a good fit.

After the initial preparation, the candidate must be ready to respond to and ask questions to show how they can benefit the organization, individuals, teams, customers, and other stakeholders.

The job description combined with research and informational discussions provides a roadmap to help anticipate the interview. Connect the needs of the buyer (the interviewer) to the capabilities of the seller (the job seeker) based on the following:

1. **Skills**
2. **Education**
3. **Work Experiences**
4. **Accomplishments**

For an effective 2-way interview, the candidate should formulate ~10-15 questions reflecting their interest and research. There may not be time to ask them all, but it's best to be ready. By asking thoughtful questions, the candidate shows interest, determination, and preparation. Some questions can be jotted down during the exchange, as relevant points will come up during the dialogue.

In responding to questions, the candidate should reference specific versus hypothetical experiences based on the following.

1. **Challenge – What was the activity, issue, or situation?**
2. **Goals – What was the mission and objectives?**
3. **Steps – What strategy and tactics were used to achieve success?**
4. **Outcome – What measurable or qualitative results took place?**

Using this approach, you can position your strengths to the opportunity. If you do not understand a question, ask for clarification. Keep the responses brief (under 2 minutes). Listen carefully and offer enough details to provide a thoughtful answer. Practice your interview responses with a friend, mentor, or career professional.

These techniques will help reduce the stress of the interview and become easier over time.

Additional tips for success:

1. **Ask relevant questions during the interview, where it makes sense in the flow of the discussion, instead of waiting until the end.**
2. **It is important to be aware of the time during an interview; use the last 5-10 minutes to understand the employer's interview process and suggest scheduling a next step (if possible).**
3. **Show genuine interest. If you like the job say in your own words that you will be "inspired to have this position with this great organization and team and look forward to contributing."**

For the Mentor, candidates who come to the interview ready to go, with preparation and a 2-way interview mindset, are going to provide a strong signal that they are a force to be reckoned with for the position. Conversely, applicants who have the capabilities, but rely on chance and a bit of charm, are more likely to be passed over.

Signs the interview is going well include:

1. **The interviewer asks about your interest in the job and a follow-up is scheduled.**
2. **The interviewer provides positive affirmation and confirms a next step.**
3. **The interview goes over the planned interview time and it feels right.**
4. **The interviewer introduces you to other team members.**
5. **The interviewer responds to your follow-up email in a positive way.**
6. **Salary comes up in context to your value and potential contributions.**

After the interview, send a thank you email to restate your interest and briefly remind the employer of how your value and capabilities align to their requirements.

Job Seeking Warriors recognize that the interviewer is trying to determine if they are the best candidate for the position, and at the same time they are assessing if the position is a high-quality fit. By asking thoughtful questions, they increase their chance of winning the position, as well as the ability to evaluate if they will be happy once in the position.

“ ”

If you do not know how to ask the right question, you discover nothing.

- W. Edwards Deming

28: SALARY NEGOTIATIONS

The job seeker knows that negotiating a salary is important and can be a bit uncomfortable. At the same time, maximizing one's worth within reason is extremely important.

Positioning the salary for a job starts early in the process when understanding the scope of the position. A key rule is to refrain from disclosing salary requirements or history too early and waiting until there is a firm offer. When the question about current salary and/or expectations comes up consider this type of response:

> *My first focus is on what I can contribute to the organization. My goal is to take the next step in my career in terms of my accountability and value to the organization. What is the salary range for this position?*

Keep in mind that the employer already has a salary in mind. If they provide a range that is far below an acceptable amount, then you can strategize to reshape the position to accommodate your salary objectives. However, if the salary expectations don't align, perhaps it's time to move on.

What's most important is to convince them that you are the best candidate.

To ensure fair compensation, it's important to prepare and know how much value you can offer the employer before the topic of salary comes up. A few tips:

1. **Calculate your value**
    - Consider the location, cost of living, career level, company salary stats (if available), and market average.
    - Build your case by showing specific examples of value that you have given employers.
    - Pick a salary range instead of a specific number; aim for a higher amount within reason.
    - Assess your leverage (e.g., currently employed vs. unemployed).

2. **Consider other forms of compensation**
   - Explore what is relevant such as extra vacation days, moving expenses, tuition reimbursement, 401(k) contributions, health insurance, stock options.
   - Assess how promotions, bonuses, and commissions (if applicable) work.
3. **Additional considerations**
   - Request the offer in writing.
   - Confirm the metrics of how a successful employee is evaluated for increases and how often.
   - Schedule your follow-up meeting or call before the negotiation ends.
   - Resist talking about your personal financial needs
   - Be prepared to walk away.
4. **Role play with a trusted friend, mentor, coach, or career councilor**
   - Expect some resistance – prepare responses including why you deserve the higher salary.

Once an offer is received it is best to pause and say, *"I need to think it over"* for an agreed number of days. Make it clear that you are interested.

The Mentor once coached a co-op (intern) who negotiated a full-time position and felt the offer was too low. She told the decision maker that she knew what she contributed to her prior jobs, how hard she works, and her value to other organizations where she could interview for a similar position. After hearing her brief and succinct case, they accepted her offer, and she achieved a major career victory.

Job Seeking Warriors welcome job offers and assessing the next steps in the negotiation. If the offer is fair, they can ask for a reasonable percent improvement or happily accept it. They understand it is important to maintain a calm, courteous, and accommodating attitude with a focus on creating a win for both themselves and the hiring organization, confirming a signed deal, and scheduling a start date.

“ ”

Each party should gain from the negotiation.

- Dale Carnegie

29: RECEIVING THE OFFER

Congratulations! After going through the job seeking process, you have an offer.

During the phone call or face-to-face meeting, confirm the timing to receive the written offer and any deadlines. If they do not mention salary or benefits, ask when they plan to provide these details.

Thank them verbally and in writing as they have put in a lot of time to choose you over other candidates.

Before signing or giving a verbal commitment there are a few steps to consider.

1. **Be prepared for the offer call; write down a few notes on what you will say.**
2. **Perhaps the negotiation has already taken place and you await the written offer, or plan to negotiate (as applicable) after you review the offer.**
3. **Let other potential employers know as they may want to make an offer.**
    - Decide how you will respond.
    - Draft a reply email confirming acceptance or politely declining.
    - If you accept, confirm the start date.
4. **Give a heads-up to any references that might be contacted for background checks.**
5. **Once you say yes, find out about onboarding details.**

Keep in mind that just because you receive an offer does not mean you must accept it. The goal is to identify the best match and optimize your short- and longer-term career goals.

If you need any clarifications, you should feel comfortable asking your main point of contact so that you understand all the details and eliminate unnecessary surprises.

After the employer indicates that you are the top candidate, it is possible you will be put into a holding pattern to get the final written offer. If so, be patient.

Try to schedule a follow-up meeting or call. Stay engaged. There may be a legitimate reason for the delay, such as needing to confirm a sign-off for the head count.

If there is a delay, stay positive. By now you should have rapport with the hiring manager, who ideally will advocate for you and share transparent insights on the status. Periodically without spamming (once every 2 or 3 weeks), send a very brief follow-up note sharing, for example, a relevant article (or reference to a social media post).

Until you accept, continue looking for other opportunities. Early in his career, the Mentor was one of the finalists for a sales position at a Fortune 500 company after completing a four-phase interview process. After meeting with the top economic decision maker, who had the power of final approval, he never did receive the offer. While disappoined, the Mentor learned a valuable lesson.

> If you do not get the offer, keep your head up and remember the famous quote that "when one door closes another will open."

Another time, a different Fortune 500 business flew the Mentor to Boston for a final interview with the top decision maker. The plane ran late. Traffic was backed up. The Mentor called the office to inform them of what happened, and they empathized with the situation. The interview started late. After 15 minutes, the department head who would make the final decision politely said that he had to catch a plane and need to go to his car.

The Mentor offered to walk with him to the car and continue their dialogue. He accepted and they had a wonderful professional conversation heading into the parking lot. Upon returning from the interview, the Mentor received a solid offer. The hiring manager shared that the interview went extremely well.

This experience serves as a reminder to always prepare for an interview discussion and expect the unexpected. If things do not happen as anticipated, stay positive until the decision is made and the deal is won.

Job Seeking Warriors pledge working hard and smart to become the best candidate for the respective position. They prepare by positioning their strengths and value to make an excellent impression each step of the way. This approach leads to a higher rate of success in receiving an offer over their competition.

When Job Seeking Warriors accept an offer, it is time to celebrate!

“ ”

It always seems impossible until it's done.

\- Nelson Mandela

30: PASSING IT FORWARD

Job seeking requires the support of many to achieve success. While it is important to thank and show appreciation for the many who have helped along the way, the greatest gift is to pass it forward.

Increasing response rates on informational meetings, interviews, and job offers requires the assistance and encouragement of others and cannot be accomplished alone.

After learning the Job Seeking Warriors' skillset from "The Challenges" to the "Power to Win," the best way to repay those who have helped along the journey, is to assist fellow job seekers as a lifelong principle.

Passing it forward does not require large amounts of time, money, or effort. It can be as simple as:

- Listening and encouraging the job seeker
- Responding to a job seeker's outreach by email, text, or call
- Helping them frame up and position their skills and work experiences
- Reviewing a resume, cover letter, or social media profile
- Participating in an informational meeting
- Making a thoughtful referral
- Keeping an eye out for new opportunities

The smallest gestures can make a big difference.

Once the job seeker begins to understand the playing field in a more enlightened way, they realize the importance of directing their energy in a positive direction and focusing on their convictions. By going beyond the current status quo, the job seeker can get from point A to point B.

When passing it forward, characteristics to spotlight include compassion, resilience, dedication, confidence, and courage. When these traits are developed and shared, an individual can obtain their personal power, as well as make better decisions with foresight and vision.

The Mentor remembers a time when his two children were small, and he was a high performing contributor for a Fortune 500 company. Upon being downsized with approximately ~400 others just before Christmas and New Year's, he sought help from his network, professionals, and former co-workers.

A few provided support, but many were too busy to respond to an email, answer a call, or provide any time for professional insights. As a result, the Mentor realized the value of making time, as much as possible, to provide insights, encourage next steps, and pass it forward.

> When passing it forward it is exciting to see a job seeker's incremental forward progress and to receive word when an excellent job is won.

From the job seeker's perspective, the challenge of finding an excellent, high-quality job can seem overwhelming. It's important to show them that any objective envisioned can become manageable when broken down into smaller parts. The true power of the Job Seeking Warrior is opening one's mind, going beyond fixed views, and believing that what is conceived can be achieved.

Passing it forward can happen at any time. A person looking for work can help others while they are searching.

The Mentor will often suggest actionable next steps as a result of an informational discussion and mutually pinpoint one or more priorities (aka "homework") along with an offer to reconnect within a few weeks to review progress.

A key consideration during this time is to overcome any obstacles and distractions. At the first sign of an impasse it is important to help a frustrated job seeker step back, identify the issue, remove it, or find a work-around. Then get right back on track.

When passing it forward it is exciting to see a job seeker's incremental forward progress and to receive word when an excellent job is won. For some the process may move faster, and for others it may take more time, but with steady pursuit it will happen.

Job Seeking Warriors cultivate themselves and become a model for other job seekers. By passing their knowledge, time, and expertise forward, they can empower others to achieve extraordinary outcomes.

> "
> If you can't pay it back, pay it forward.
> - Catherine Ryan Hyde

CHECKLIST

- [ ] ....
  ....
- [ ] ....
  ....
- [ ] ....
  ....

JOB SEEKING WARRIORS ACTIONABILITY NOTES

JOB SEEKING WARRIORS ACTIONABILITY NOTES

JOB SEEKING WARRIORS ACTIONABILITY NOTES

JOB SEEKING WARRIORS ACTIONABILITY NOTES

JOB SEEKING WARRIORS ACTIONABILITY NOTES

JOB SEEKING WARRIORS ACTIONABILITY NOTES

JOB SEEKING WARRIORS ACTIONABILITY NOTES

JOB SEEKING WARRIORS ACTIONABILITY NOTES

JOB SEEKING WARRIORS ACTIONABILITY NOTES

JOB SEEKING WARRIORS ACTIONABILITY NOTES

JOB SEEKING WARRIORS ACTIONABILITY NOTES

JOB SEEKING WARRIORS ACTIONABILITY NOTES

JOB SEEKING WARRIORS ACTIONABILITY NOTES

JOB SEEKING WARRIORS ACTIONABILITY NOTES

JOB SEEKING WARRIORS ACTIONABILITY NOTES

JOB SEEKING WARRIORS ACTIONABILITY NOTES

JOB SEEKING WARRIORS ACTIONABILITY NOTES

JOB SEEKING WARRIORS ACTIONABILITY NOTES

ACKNOWLEDGMENTS

Writing this book has been more rewarding than I ever could have imagined. Most of all I would like to thank my wife, Sharon, for her incredible inspiration throughout the journey and encouragement to turn thousands of experiences into a book.

A very special thank you to my daughter, Lauren, and son, Steven, who proved that these skillsets work by applying them in their own career pursuits.

In memory of my parents, Harris and Grace, who instilled many lessons, and would have enjoyed reading this book.

My appreciation to my mother-in-law Beverly Feldman, who encouraged me and believed in this journey.

To my many friends and colleagues at Drexel University who have teamed and collaborated on many job seeking, career, and professional development programs. Thank you for the many lessons learned and experiences along the way.

A special thanks to my WSS team both current and past who have made an enormous impact on my professional and personal life including Jenny Ly Cao, Erin McHugh and along the way Rachel Granger, Elizabeth Griesser, Diem Lam, and Elle Savage as well as all the awesome Drexel co-op students who teamed with us and continued forward on their career journeys.

To Brad Borkan, co-author of "When Your Life Depends on It" and "Audacious Goals, Remarkable Results" who shared insights on the art and science of writing a book, which helped me realize the many key steps along the way.

ABOUT THE AUTHOR

RICHARD D. BLUMBERG is the president of World Sales Solutions, LLC (WSS), a leading business development and collaboration technology consulting firm. He and his team consult with SAP, the world's largest business software company, the SAP ecosystem, and Fortune 1000 organizations. He is a Drexel Alumni Board of Governors Emeritus.

For over two decades he has provided volunteer job seeking, career, and professional development mentoring and coaching in one-to-one meetings and group sessions for thousands of students, recent graduates, and seasoned alumni.

He holds a five-year co-operative education Bachelor of Science degree in Business Administration for Marketing from Drexel University and resides in Montgomery Township, Pennsylvania.

You are invited to continue your experience with JOB SEEKING WARRIORS on our website.

Share your job seeking challenges and experiences.
Find out what others are saying.
Engage the author.
Download templates and example resources.
Read blogs and other updates.
Purchase additional copies.

www.JobSeekingWarriors.com

Learn about having the author speak to your organization or group.

Made in the USA
Monee, IL
20 October 2022

16243353R00079